THE DAILY STUDY BIBLE SERIES
REVISED EDITION

THE GOSPEL OF
MATTHEW

Volume 2